Attention All Staff!

"Attention All Staff!"

Ten Camp Emergencies with Commentary

by

Bo Shoemaker, M.A., J.D., LL.M.
Camp Historian, YMCA Camp Cory

Illustrations by Bill Smith
Digital conversions and editing by Dave Ghidiu

Rochester, NY

To camp people everywhere

I have been so inured to difficulties in the course of this contest that I have learned to look on them with more tranquility than formerly.

- George Washington

Table of Contents

Introduction

It's a beautiful July day. You have a few free minutes to yourself while you walk across your camp. Things are quieter than usual – one of your largest villages is on a canoeing trip to a nearby park for a lunchtime cookout. The other activities are all running smoothly. You're just about to head back to your office for some paperwork when you hear a call from over the walkie-talkie.

The call is from one of your Village Heads. He is leading his fifty-or-so campers back from the park, in their canoes, and has made a terrifying realization: he has two fewer campers than he should. You grab the Waterfront Coordinator and your Waterski Coordinator, hop into the ski-boat, and jet out to where the Village Director is paddling the lead canoe. He shouts that he's since counted all of his kids again and is still two campers short.

A minute passes while you count the campers yourself. The canoes are beginning to beach at your camp, and the campers are wondering where to go. None of the counselors from the village seem to notice any particular camper missing. The Village Head swears he's two short. Your Waterfront Coordinator is wondering if he should prepare to conduct a deep-water search drill. He is already going over the procedures to himself. Your Office Manager keeps fervently calling you over the walkie-talkie. Should she send the driver out somewhere? Should she call the Sheriff? What do you do?

***

Whether once or a dozen times every summer, at some point every camp will go into "crisis mode."

This collection of retellings, with commentary, seeks to differentiate between the several types of emergencies, and to recommend methods for dealing with them. I postulate there are four general types of emergencies that a camp (or indeed, any organization) may face. Emergencies that are oft-encountered should be responded-to with well-practiced procedures that are largely automatic. Otherwise, the best way to respond to one emergency is to have a leader present who has already responded to many.

I would be remiss if I did not acknowledge the assistance I received from Camp Cory staff members, both former and current. A very special thanks are owed to Dave Ghidiu, Aaron Weaver, Greg Casto, and Brian Dana, who provided many additional details, recommendations, and suggestions. And, of course, I must thank Bill Smith for his wonderful illustrations.

Several of the chapters contain contemporaneous journal entries and incident reports. For this reason, please excuse colloquialisms,

vagueness, and bracketed additions. Read on – I hope
it will be with interest.

Chapter 1:

<u>The Water Backboarding Incident</u>

NOTE: The following documents were created and compiled, collectively, within 24 hours of the incident they describe.

August 4, 2009

YMCA Camp Cory – Sailing Incident Report

SUMMARY:

A JY-15 capsized and a camper required rescue. She was backboarded and placed on the party boat. The party boat drove in, EMS personnel took over care, and the camper was transported to the hospital. Meanwhile, high winds and waves affected all other sailboats, motorboats, and the rescue operation itself.

NICOLE ECKER, MAIJGREN VILLAGE HEAD:

Nicole was driving the party boat, Kali Adriaansen was boat crew, and Adam Falk was shore crew. Kali had jumped out of the party boat to help out Dan Drabiak's boat, because they couldn't right it. Nicole saw that Mark Dibble and Chris Mattle pulled up to the JY, so Nicole proceeded to other boats (there were three or four down at the time). When Nicole was helping Caitlin Broman's boat, [a] jetskier drove up to the party boat.

He said that there was an unconscious sailor at one of the downed JY15s, and that Nicole should follow him to the boat. Nicole drove as fast as possible to the capsized craft. Duncan had Caleigh up on the boat, keeping her head out of the water. Nicole jumped in with a tube and noticed that Caleigh was unconscious. Within 10 seconds of Nicole yelling her name, Caleigh woke up. Nicole asked if she knew her name: Caleigh knew her first name, and it took her about 5 seconds to answer about her last name. She couldn't think of her father's or brothers' name. She kept not speaking for a while, so Nicole asked her to sing the ABCs. She got to "D" and then stopped.

Nicole took Caleigh's hand and had her squeeze. Nicole also had Caleigh push her feet against Duncan to ensure that she had lower-body capabilities. Nicole let Caleigh rest her head on Nicole's lifejacket, because it was better floatation and because she assumed that, because of the responsiveness of all of Caleigh's limbs, in-line stabilization was no longer necessary.

Nicole asked the jetskier to get the Yamaha, which Nicole thought had Mark and Mattle in it, but actually had Mattle and Kali, and for them to bring the backboard. Kali eventually arrived, via the jetskier, with the backboard. Mattle then arrived with the Yamaha and got on the party boat, leaving the Yamaha adrift. The jetskier then left, on his own recognizance, to talk to someone at camp [the Jr.

Waterfront]. Caleigh had passed out again for about

ten seconds or so, so Nicole and Kali put Caleigh on

the backboard, Duncan assisting with retrieving the

straps. The jetskier then arrived with Claudette

Crowley, and put her on the party boat.

When Caleigh woke up again, Nicole asked

what her name was, *et cetera*, and Caleigh knew she

was at camp and knew her name, but it took her a

while to think that she had been sailing just before

then. Nicole told Caleigh that they were putting her

on a backboard and that she wouldn't be able to move

her body. This upset Caleigh. After 3 or 4 minutes,

the party boat maneuvered to a position, relative to

those in the water, where extraction would be

practicable. Nicole remained with Caleigh in the

water while Kali and Duncan got onto the party boat.

Then the jetskier jumped in to help Nicole.

They lifted her onto the party boat incorrectly

(Nicole was at the head of the board, and those on the

party boat lifted it from the side of the board. Lifters were Kali, Duncan, and Claudette). Once Caleigh was on the party boat, Claudette started to check her. The jetskier and Nicole got onto the jetski and Nicole was about to head back to the turtled (Oliver and Matt's) JY. Party boat submarined a couple times (it had been submarining a couple times even with Nicole there by herself), while Mark, Pat, Bo, and Adam arrived in the ski boat. (Caleigh had been on the party boat for less than 30 seconds when Mark, et. al., arrived).

Nicole got onto the ski boat, jetskier left, Adam and Bo got on the Yamaha, and Nicole went in with Mark and Pat. The ski boat caught up to the party boat and docked before the [latter]. Nicole brought blankets to cover Caleigh, who was shivering. Then Nicole rested.

Chris Mattle and Mark took the Yamaha out. They were driving around, waiting for someone to come in on a JY so that they could go sailing. Boats were tipping, and Mark would drive over to check on them. Kids were fine, and were having fun. At Dan Drabiak's boat, Kali was helping him right it. Nicole had dropped her there and had gone to check on another boat. Dan was asking for a tow in, and Mark didn't want to tow a JY in (it probably would have flipped anyways in that heavy water). Mark was going to sail in, and it flipped again before Mark could get to it. Dan asked to tow it upside-down. Mark told Chris to drive the Yamaha with Kali in it. Mark entered the water, helped right the boat, and sailed it in.

When Mark got to the beach, things were a little hectic. People were telling him that there was a boat over, that it needed EMS, that it needed a backboard, et cetera. Adam was trying to radio to figure out what was going on, but Nicole had stopped answering the radio. Adam handed the radio off to Pat. Mark was on the Y dock, and Adam came out and said he felt like he should be out there. Adam said that Sarah Wallace, Kara Maillie, and Alex Stirling could watch the shore. However, Alex was in Outdoor Education and Sarah was the nanny, so it was really just Kara. Mark said he was not comfortable with Adam coming, because emergencies tend to happen in other areas when they are not supervised properly. Adam begrudgingly understood. Mark then saw Theresa Civiletti swimming a JY around the dock, and Mark said that this was exactly what he meant, that Kara didn't know this was going on. Steve Haynes came over in the ski boat, with Pat and Bo, and Mark asked Steve to get out and watch the shore.

***

After Bo and Adam were dropped off on the Yamaha, Mark and Pat, in the ski boat, got to the Y

Dock, alongside or near the party boat. Mark watched Claudette take vitals of Caleigh. Brian Dana's boat came in, docked, and the kids went [towards] the Sr. Boathouse. One kid started leading the rest of the kids, and Kali yelled "Go to the Sr. Boathouse!"

[A staff member], at one point, was sobbing pretty heavily, and Adam took her for a walk. The sheriff showed up, and said that without the ambulance he couldn't really do anything other than radio in more information.

Bo Shoemaker, Senior Program Director:

I was in the Program Office when [Waterfront Director] Beth Clemson radioed me. She stated that a jetskier had just come to the dock, claiming that the Party Boat had told him that there was a situation out on the water that required EMS. [Leadership Director] Pat Foster and I grabbed lifejackets and headed down to the sailing waterfront. Adam Falk was helping campers get into and out of JY-15s, and knew nothing of this situation. Mark was sailing a JY-15 in, and he, too, knew nothing of this. Pat informed Adam and Mark of what Beth had told us, and then Pat and I started walking over to the Junior Waterfront in order to get the ski boat. Mark asked us to pick him up at the Y dock once we got the boat.

I attempted to radio the party boat and have them check on all of the sailboats – I assumed that there was a possibility that a boat was over with an injured camper, and that the party boat didn't know about it. I had some trouble contacting anyone through the radio, but then I got a brief response from Chris Mattle that "[we have a] backboard situation" on the water.

The Junior Waterfront was already cleared of campers, and Caitlin and Beth repeated the backboard-related information that I had heard before. Steve Haynes approached in the ski boat, full of campers, and we had him empty the boat of the campers. Pat and I joined Steve – I had Steve remain as driver because I figured he would be the most confident and competent driver of that particular boat.

We drove by the Y dock, picked up Mark and Adam Falk, and Mark asked Steve to stay with the village. I saw Theresa Civiletti swimming her boat around the Y-Dock, and Mark said to Adam, "This is exactly what I mean." Blake Martin and Caitlin Lohrberg sprinted down the boardwalk, for no apparent reason, and Brandon Decker yelled at kids to get off the dock.

Mark drove the ski boat out to where the party boat was located. Nicole screamed to us, "She passed out at least three times…" and started shouting some more. I looked over to the party boat. Chris Mattle was driving, and Kali Adriaansen and Claudette Crowley were standing over Caleigh Sullivan, who was lying on the backboard. Duncan Jagel was, apparently, on the boat, although I don't remember seeing him at the time. All except Mattle were on the bow of the boat, outside the cabin.

The waves were so large that one of them overtook the bow, and that part of the boat was briefly submerged. Adam Falk commented that the party boat was submarining, but by that time Chris Mattle had already gone into reverse and had stabilized the boat. The jetskier said that the staff members might need help moving Caleigh into the cabin of the boat, but we noticed that they had already moved her. We thanked the jetskier for his help, and he drove away.

Mark dropped Adam and myself off at the Yamaha boat, which was adrift. I was able to get only the right engine started, but we were able to limp over to another capsized sailboat. Adam jumped in to help them sail in, and I drove the Yamaha back to shore. Steve Haynes and I transported Maijgren campers off of the two J-24s and to the Junior Dock. They waited in the Arts & Crafts Lodge.

Finally, when Caleigh was ready to move, Pat Foster and I assisted in carrying the backboard [with Caleigh on it] up to the parking lot. EMS moved Caleigh to a stretcher, and then left for the hospital. Afterwards, Duncan Jagel, Oliver Vitale, and Matt Montella were interviewed by Yates County Sheriff's deputies. Pat and I sat with Duncan for most of his questioning, at the Maijgren picnic table, and Adam Falk was standing near Oliver and Matt, in the Maijgren gazebo.

KALI ADRIAANSEN, SENIOR COUNSELOR:

Kali was on boat crew. Many boats were capsizing and turtling. Dan Drabiak's boat was unable to right, and Kali was in the water helping them to right, but it kept going back over. Mark Dibble eventually jumped in to help, and Kali got back on the Yamaha. There was another boat that had been capsized for a couple minutes. Kali and Chris Mattle drove over to help that boat. That boat said that they were O.K., but that someone else was hurt, so Kali and Mattle drove to get to the party boat. Nicole, Duncan, and Caleigh were in the water, and Nicole said that they needed the backboard. Chris Mattle grabbed on to the party boat. Kali got the backboard, got into the water, and a good Samaritan jetskier pulled Kali over to Nicole, with the backboard. Nicole said that it wasn't a spinal or head injury, and they started strapping Caleigh in.

Kali removed the guard tube after Caleigh was strapped in. They talked to Caleigh the whole time because she was panicking. The straps on the backboard were clipped, so Kali had to reach under and un-clip them. Kali swam back to the party boat and climbed on to the deck. Jetskier arrived with Claudette, the nurse. Kali, Claudette, and Duncan pulled the backboard onto the bow of the boat. The

boat headed back towards camp, nose-diving a little,

and the staff moved Caleigh back farther into the

cabin of the boat. Staff kept talking to Caleigh as

Claudette was working on her.

They got back to shore, Kali grabbed the bow

line and pulled the boat to the dock. Kali told Nicole

to get a blanket because she, Nicole, was soaked. Kali

then headed to the Sr. Boathouse to be with the kids.

DUNCAN JAGEL, MAIJGREN CAMPER:

Heavy wind, from the south, so the waves were

pretty big. Earlier, Duncan had been out and would

get hit by rogue waves. That would cause the boat to

capsize right away.

The boat in the instant case had tacked, and as

the sails were filling up, a wave hit the boat. The boat

capsized. The boom hit Duncan in the head. Caleigh

fell and her head hit the gunwale, so Duncan asked if

she was O.K. She mumbled and rolled over so that her face was in the water. Duncan pulled her out away from the boat, because it was clear that the boat would turtle. Both of her legs were caught in the main sheet, so Duncan had to go underwater to unwrap the sheet from her legs. Once they swam past the rudder, Duncan's foot got caught in the main sheet, but he was able to kick it off. It was at this point that Duncan discovered that Caleigh was unconscious.

Duncan was not sure if Caleigh was alive. He swam around the boat, holding Caleigh's head above the water, and grabbed the gunwale. He told Ollie and Matt to get onto the boat and start waving their arms. He told them that Caleigh was unconscious. Duncan checked her pulse, and felt one, and leaned in to feel her breath, and she was still breathing.

Because of the waves, Duncan was unable to hold her next to him – the waves would wash over her face. He put Caleigh on his knee and kicked with his right leg to keep her above the water, while keeping

her up with his left hand, which was behind her neck.

He waited in this position for 7 or 8 minutes. A

jetskier came by, and Duncan told him that there was

an unconscious camper, and that the jetskier should go

get the party boat.

Shortly after the jetskier left, Caleigh woke up

and was complaining about a pain in her head and

neck. Then she passed out again. Nicole showed up

on the party boat, jumped in with her guard tube.

Nicole awoke Caleigh for a few minutes, but Caleigh

passed out shortly before the party boat arrived.

Nicole put the tube under Caleigh's back, and Nicole

and Duncan kept Caleigh pointed towards the waves.

They sat for 3 or 4 minutes while they waited for Chris

and Kali.

Kali and Chris arrived. Kali jumped in the

water, and Nicole told her that the backboard was in

the party boat. Then she climbed onto the party boat,

jumped in with the backboard, and the jetskier went back to get the nurse. While he was leaving, Duncan, Kali, and Nicole got Caleigh onto the backboard, put in the head blocks, and couldn't work the jaw strap, so didn't use it but kept the jaw strap on, dangling. Kali climbed onto the party boat, Chris helping her. The party boat drifted away during this time, and Duncan and Nicole held the backboard. (Duncan slipped the tube underneath where Caleigh's head was, on the backboard).

Duncan got onto the party boat, and Duncan, Kali, and Chris pulled the backboard up onto the party boat (nurse was there, but didn't pull). Now 5 were on the party boat. Caleigh was conscious for her duration on the party boat. The bow dipped, water rushing over Caleigh's head, so they picked her up and moved her towards the center of the boat. Kali slipped, letting go with one hand. Duncan had to put his arm on the other side to carry most of the weight over the railing.

From there, the nurse checked Caleigh, and the party boat got back to camp. At the dock, Duncan removed the blocks, and Caleigh was fully conscious at this point. Paramedics and sheriff arrived. They cut off Caleigh's necklace and removed her lifejacket. They attached a collar, the nurse rechecked blood pressure and pulse, and then the blocks were put back in place, strapped her head in.

CLAUDETTE CROWLEY, CAMP NURSE:

4:15 pm, called to the waterfront for an assist with a camper in the water. Taken by jetski to the pontoon boat. Camper Caleigh Sullivan was on backboard with head blocks intact. Rescue swimmers were with her in the water. She was lifted onto the front of the pontoon deck. She was alert, following simple commands, and shivering. She was covered with towels and sweatshirts.

Water washed over the front of the boat. She was picked up on the backboard and moved to the center of the boat. Vital signs: heart rate 100, respiratory rate 24, bp 100/80, neuro check was done [PERRLA: pupils are equal, round, react to light, accommodating]. Moving all extremities well. Bilateral grips equal. Oriented x3 (who, where, when).

Repeated vital sign check every few minutes. Heart 100, resp. 24, bp 110/70. Transported to the docks via pontoon boat. Remained alert and shivering. Once at the docks blankets were placed on Caleigh. Vital signs stable. Neuro check done. Alert and oriented x3. States her butt hurts due to prior tailbone injury this week. EMS met on the boat. Transferred care to EMS, report given. Transported to hospital via ambulance.

ADAM FALK, SAILING MASTER:

Pat and Bo came down the stairs next to the Yacht Club. Pat told Adam that a jetskier had come to Beth and told her to call EMS. Mark had just arrived on a JY, and Mark radioed the party boat to go to other boats. But contact with the party boat was not possible at the time. Adam thought that possibly the jetskier had just overreacted.

When Mark and Adam couldn't reach the party boat, Adam got on a lifejacket. Adam and Mark hopped into the ski boat once it arrived. Adam witnessed Caleigh on the backboard, the party boat nose-diving, Adam and Bo then transferred to the Yamaha. Adam was dropped off at Ollie Vitale and Matt Montella's JY and helped them to sail it in.

CHRIS MATTLE, VISITOR
(former Wells Village Head, Maijgren Village Head, and Sailing Master):

Mark and Chris were in the Yamaha motorboat. Kali Adriaansen was already in the water helping a turtled JY-15 (there were three total), and Mark got in to help them. Chris Mattle was to take Kali back to the party boat in the Yamaha. In the meantime, the party boat, which was at another capsized boat, had been flagged down by a jetski.

The second JY told the Yamaha that the party boat had gone to the third JY, and that there was a problem. Party boat was adrift near the third JY. Yamaha pulled alongside, and Nicole said that they wanted the backboard from the party boat. Yamaha went back over to get it. Mattle figured they couldn't backboard onto the Yamaha, and that the party boat was better. Mattle told Kali to get onto the party boat, and she said she wasn't clear to drive it. Mattle: "It doesn't fucking matter!"

Mattle jumped onto the party boat, leaving the Yamaha adrift. Kali grabbed the backboard and jumped off the party boat. A jetskier pulled Kali over

to the JY. The party boat pulled up to the accident.

Mattle couldn't figure out the radio. He told the

jetskier to head in to shore and tell them that we

needed EMS.

Mattle stayed nearby while backboarding

occurred. Staff members put Caleigh on the boat. The

boat dipped face-first into the water briefly, and then

the boat drove to the Y-dock. EMS was there.

Everyone was happy and fine and good.

***

Commentary:

This was a fairly atypical crisis not because it

was unexpected and fast-paced, but because of its

scale: it quickly subsumed the entire camp. Because

the waterfront and waterfront activities make up such

a large part of what Camp Cory does, the severity of

the weather affected the scale and scope of the

emergency. Land-based activities were quickly halted or converted into triage-type zones, in which staff members took in wayward waterfront campers, supervised them, kept them calm, kept them busy.

As the waterfront campers were filtered into land zones, water-based staff were gradually given more and more freedom to respond to the emergency. This was beneficial, since the waterfront staff members in 2009, especially those on Central Staff, tended to have a degree of expertise in boats and lifeguarding skills. They moreover tended to have in that year a fair amount of experience responding to emergencies of all types. Indeed, several members of the Central Staff (generally those with "Director" in their titles) had been working at camp for nearly a decade. Several, too, had Master's Degrees, although I am not sure whether and to what extent that affected the situation.[1]

____

[1] Update for the paperback version: *but see* Laz's take on the Barkley

Those staff members (including in this case a former staff member) with much experience dealing with emergencies had veritable grimoires of disaster-response prescriptions at their disposal. For example, someone with years of experience as a village head, sailing instructor, and lifeguard had seen many emergencies and had previously been required to respond to them. If he could keep his wits about him this time around, he would know what works, what doesn't, where things went wrong last time, what he would have done differently last time (and could change now), and would hopefully also have a more innate and ingrained understanding of procedures that are supposed to be largely automatic (for example, lifeguarding rescue maneuvers). In short, an experienced emergency responder has common sense,

<hr>

Marathons ultramarathon runners in the film *The Race that Eats its Young*. Most of the runners are acclaimed professionals with advanced degrees . . . they have succeeded all throughout their life by setting goals and following through with hard work and focus. "We have such a high number of people [i.e. runners] that have graduate degrees because they set goals, they accomplish them, they don't let anything stand in their way."

has learned by trial-and-error, and is not as easily overcome by panic and stress because he or she has seen these types of things so many times before.

This disaster is also a helpful study because of the number of staff members involved. Some of them were extremely experienced, some of them only marginally so, and a few of them had little to no experience. Some of the rescuers panicked, some of them made quick but nevertheless faulty decisions, and some of them seemed to know exactly what to do.

This emergency had quite a bit of panic at its inception. Staff on the shore, the ones with the most experience, were left confused for several minutes while things developed out on the water. The best course of action would have been to immediately radio to shore in order to get the emergency action plan mechanisms moving. The extra ten seconds this communication would have taken would most likely not have adversely affected the situation out on the water, especially given that it would have resulted in alerting everyone sooner. I have found (and I hope these emergencies will illustrate) that situations in which *literally* every second matters are extremely rare. A good course of action is to take the 5 or 10 seconds that are necessary to calm down, think things over, and certainly to alert others to the existence of an emergency (this also has the added benefit of stemming the tide of spreading panic).

You will also notice that there was some premature entry into the water (due to panicking) and the leaving of motorboats adrift (possibly due to panicking). The actual rescue of the camper in the water was not carried out according to Red Cross or, to my knowledge, YMCA standards (I know of no "paralysis test" where a potential spinal victim is asked to press her feet or hands against her rescuer). Some staff members also yelled at children in order to direct them, which was probably unnecessary and had the potential for making the situation worse by increasing the level of tension and the impression of chaos.

Immediately after the emergency was over, Camp Director Mark Dibble asked me to chronicle what had happened so that we could get some overall idea of the situation. By around breakfast the following day I had completed my interviews (Claudette had made handwritten notes on her own that she read to me as I typed them down). I neglected to interview my fellow Program Director Aaron Weaver – he apparently was quite active in organizing the entire land-based response to the emergency. Him being left in charge of all non-water activities was for the best: he probably lacked the level of water expertise that some other staff members had, but had worked at camp and had responded to emergencies there for a decade. Moreover, he was studying emergency medicine at the University of Rochester (he is now an emergency room doctor) and thus had specialized knowledge and general level-headedness that proved invaluable to the land-based response and coordination with the medical authorities. (The injured camper recovered, was discharged that same day, and returned to camp that evening, after apparently stopping for some ice cream).

I still vividly remember coming to the Y-dock with Mark and Adam Falk standing there, seeing a camper swimming a boat around the dock, and Mark telling Adam "this is exactly what I mean." I didn't find out until my post-emergency interviews what he had meant. The land people, the triage people, the people who should be making sure everything else stays status quo, were either overwhelmed or were panicking themselves. Mark's decision to keep some experience on shore seems to have been the right one. Otherwise, things can rapidly deteriorate, and more emergencies can easily arise.

In a situation like this, where there is surprise and where there is no time to plan, decision-making should contract and become vertical. The highest authority there (the most experienced, hopefully) is the person who is most likely to make correct decisions. The further down the chain, the less experience, the greater the possibility for panic. I thought Steve Haynes would have been the best choice as ski-boat driver, but it was good that I didn't question Mark's decision to leave Steve in charge of the village, because Mark was the highest leader.

I believe that, at the beginning of the emergency, Pat Foster and I began running towards the Waterfront. But I quickly put a stop to that because a running staff member, especially a running Central Staff member, puts people on edge and, again, increases tension and chaos. The relative calm is almost always worth the extra few seconds it takes to get somewhere.

One last thing of note: after the crisis was over, there was a whole-staff debriefing. Several staff members wanted policies put in place, plans made, exercises to practice. Mark rightfully explained that those were not necessary. What he didn't say was, not only were they not necessary, but they would be both futile and folly. This particular brand of emergency would probably never happen again while these staff members were working at camp. The best course of action with fast-paced, unexpected emergencies, as stated above, is to simply have everyone obey commands from the highest-level authority.

Chapter 2:

Inter-Camp Relations

The Camp Cory online email account received this message around the Spring of 2009:

E-mail Address: [xxxx]@netscape.net

Elmira, NY 14903

Branch: CampCory

Question: Hi! I work at Camp Iroquois and i was wondering if there were any way we could compete at anything during the summer.. it would make both camps way more fun. at the same time i see a problem brewing.. theres no way to get the campers in this.. theres just too many of them.

but im thinking on a weekend or something.
maybe a capture the flag game at
iroquois.. a regatta from your camp to
ours.. and something else.. the winner
being the camp with most points gets a
trophy of some sort.. it would keep
couselors at camp for the weekend and
would be a great time.. we could have a
cookout or something after.. just an
idea.. I know we haven't been good
'neighbors' so to say but a little
competition every summer could help fix
that.. camp for me is the time of my
life.. im just looking to make it better
for years to come.. maybe some more
friends from a 'rival' camp would help to
relieve some tensions.. its worth a shot
right??

***

Camp Director Mark Dibble forwarded the message on to me, and asked what my thoughts were on the matter. I was entering into my second summer as Program Director. Here was my response to Mark:

> *Based on their behavior the past few summers I can see this turning ugly really easily.*
>
> *The only time, I think, to do a staff-only thing would be staff week, and I'm not sure we want to start off on that foot.*
>
> *And as for doing something with our campers and their campers, I don't think we ever want to go on that foot this summer. Maybe if we've had a*

*... Mark asked me to respond to Brendan in any way I
saw fit...*

Brendan,

Thank you for your recommendation; I
agree that competition between camps
can provide a constructive outlet for
competitive instincts and can give
campers a new perspective on other
camps. There are, however, some
concerns with some of the aspects of
your proposal, and with the recent
conduct of Camp Iroquois staff in
particular, that preclude us from
such a competition with your camp
this coming summer.

First, I believe that any competition
would have to involve campers. We
try to make any programming that goes
on during our season camper-focused.
The only time that staff would be
able to compete in such an event
would be during a weekend or during
our Staff Training Week. On
weekends, we still run programs for
stayover campers for which they may
need use of the boats. Moreover,
staff who have the weekend off will
most likely want to take that time
off for themselves, and it would be
extremely difficult to coax them to
stay at camp for a non-camper-related
event. During our Staff Training

Week, too, we are focused primarily on childcare training, the philosophy of camp counseling, and social bonding between our staff members. We would hesitate to engage in any activity that would take time away from this training with little or no professional or social benefit in return.

Second, for any competition to take place involving campers, we would need to be comfortable that it would be a valuable experience for them, and that the benefits of the competition would far outweigh the risks presented by inappropriate behavior and poor examples set by staff.

Which brings me to my third concern: you are correct in pointing out that the relationship between our two camps has been noticeably strained for the past few years. In fact, it has been that way for the tenure of my employment at Camp Cory. I realize that a level of competition between camps is traditional in some places, and while I understand that you are not personally responsible for the behavior of your fellow staff members, it is nevertheless the case that our campers and staff have been legitimately angered and distressed by some of the actions committed by your camp. So that you may have a better idea of our feelings on this matter, I've included some examples from only the past few years:

In 2006, members of the Camp Iroquois staff broke into one of our buildings, the Yacht Club, during preseason. While there, they attempted to goad our staff into a regatta by writing a note in one of our administrative notebooks. That same summer, in response to a good faith effort on our part to retrieve property that had been stolen during a previous summer, representatives from Camp Iroquois boarded one of our moored boats at night and placed a pair of underwear on the halyard.

In 2007, our sailing village took an overnight trip to Bluff Point. During the night, representatives from Camp Iroquois stole food from our beached boats, thereby preventing our campers from having a meal on their return trip.

In 2008, while our sailing village was on a similar overnight trip to Bluff Point, representatives from Camp Iroquois harassed and threatened a group of our campers and staff who were hiking down a road. Our campers were legitimately afraid, and we seriously contemplated involving the legal authorities. Later on in the summer, staff members from Camp Iroquois removed our camp's sign and concealed it, resulting in irreparable damage to the sign.

I do wish that our camps could engage in friendlier affairs, but given recent history I think it unlikely to

*happen soon. I would be too worried
that, at any event between our two
camps, our campers and staff would be
subjected to the same behavior that
they were in 2008, which would be
completely unacceptable.*

*I am glad that you want things to
change, and I hope you and your
fellow staff members can prove me
wrong. Given a few incident-free
summers, our camp will reconsider
competing with yours, as we currently
compete with Camp Seneca Lake. But
for this coming summer,
unfortunately, we must decline.
Please feel free to pass this along
to anyone at Camp Iroquois, and to
respond with any other questions or
concerns you might have.*

Very truly yours,

*Bo Shoemaker
Senior Program Director, YMCA Camp
Cory*

***

<u>Bluff Trip, Tuesday, July 14th, 2009</u>

<u>Typed by Bo Shoemaker</u>

41

James Fester:

As he was driving the camp truck down the hill towards the campsite, he passed many staff and campers from Camp Iroquois. They said things like,

- "We know who you are, Cory."
- "You hippies."
- "We know where you sleep."
- "You can't hide from us."

Bo Shoemaker:

As I was trying to park the van on the side of the road, near the campsite, an Iroquois staff member stood in my way nonchalantly. I went down the trail to talk to Adam Falk and Nicole, and told them to just ignore Camp Iroquois, and to be wary at night, and to keep the keys to the truck. When I was coming back up the hill, I saw a Camp Iroquois camper defecating on the trail. He quickly pulled up his pants and ran to the road, nearby, where his counselor was waiting for him. The two of them then walked up the hill together, towards the Garrett Chapel.

ADAM FALK:

Camp Iroquois boats apparently (second-hand) came up to the Cory boats and said stuff about "rich kids" and "Cory sucks."

Second-hand: Iroquois people were forming a line up at the road, talking to the Cory people on the road, saying stuff like, "you're sleeping in our poo." While this was happening, Adam was at the campsite, down the hill, making the fire. Village Head Nicole Ecker was up at the road with the CITs, and campers were moving food from the road to the campsite.

Estimates a dozen kids defecated on the trail (about 12 different piles, with used toilet paper nearby).

The next day, on the return trip, one of the Iroquois motorboats came out and was "recklessly" [in the colloquial sense] circling one of the K-Boats.

(Possibly Kali Adriaansen's boat). Adam actually

heard them saying "Cory sucks." The Iroquois staff

were adults, with younger campers on their boats.

They called Adam and Nicole "hippies," and called the

rest of the kids "rich kids." While harassing Matt

Smith's boat, they almost hit him.

***

NICOLE ECKER:

About ten minutes after the van left (so, ~7 pm),

Nicole went up to the road and there were Iroquois

campers and staff standing about a step off the trail,

peeing off into the woods. Nicole stayed up at the

road. Matt Smith, Tim Casto, and Grace Leone came

up the hill, making 4 Cory personnel present. Camp

Iroquois then started coming down the hill, dozens in

number. Jake Snyder, a volunteer and former

waterfront director at Iroquois, came down the hill and

introduced Nicole to the camp director, Dave. Dave

told Nicole that he can't really control what his staff and kids do, but if we'd like to retaliate, that's fine. Possibly: "Well, my staff and kids will do what they want. But if you would like to retaliate, that's fine with us." Dave then left, and some of the older male Iroquois counselors started coming down and saying that they were going to pee on the trail. The four Coryites said that it was private property and that the Iroquois staff couldn't do that. The Coryites stood in their way, an Iroquois staff member said, "Oh yes we can," and tried to go around. Nicole reiterated that it was private property and that they should get off. Then the Iroquois staff started to chant, "You sleep where we poop," or possibly, "You sleep where we shit." Then the Iroquois staff left.

Nicole saw only the one pile of feces, with the used toilet paper strewn on a branch nearby.

Nicole did hear some voices in the middle of the night, but it cannot be confirmed that it was anyone from their camp.

On Cory's return trip, Iroquois started to rig as soon as it was in sight of the Cory boats. When the Cory boats were about 300 feet away, they, Iroquois, launched their sailboats. Then a large motorboat, filled with kids, drove in circles around one of the K-boats (skippered by Evan Zeise). One of the sailboats went over to one or more of the Cory boats, yelling things like, "Rich kids, learn how to sail. Why don't you let the kids sail?" (Kali Adriaansen was on that boat). The Iroquois staff member on the sailboat kept shouting something like, "I'll see you tonight," to the Cory staff and campers. Then he said to Nicole, "I'll see you later tonight, sweetheart."

Text message sent to Nicole at 9:21 am, Wednesday, from Jake Snyder, "Should we call the state police too since that's what you were going to do?

If you want a was [sic] we'll give you one!" [This text was probably sent around when the Cory boats were passing Camp Iroquois.] [Nicole speculates that the "police" idea came because at this time Adam Falk took out his phone to call Mark Dibble].

***

Evan Zeise:

Camp Iroquois boat circled his boat, said nothing, and waved.

***

Matt Brennan:

On the way down, Camp Iroquois staff were on Hobies and called the Cory people "hippies." "Hey hippies, how's rich camp going?" They said, "Those look slow," in regards to the K-boats. "See ya at the bluff, rich kids."

On the way back, the same staff member on a Hobie said, "Wow, only Camp Cory would do running free for six miles down the lake, you guys are idiots."

47

"How's rich camp going for ya?" Matt Smith was steering for a little bit, and the man said, "Oh, the counselors have to steer? Did the campers not pay enough to steer yet?" [Nicole and Matt would both recognize the man if they saw him. He was the one who said the "sweetheart" line.]

***

Commentary:

Camp Iroquois is a bastard camp located on the eastern side of the Bluff on Keuka Lake. It is run by the New York State Sheriffs' Association for at-risk youth. It used to be run by the Elmira YMCA, so of old it and Camp Cory, run by the Rochester YMCA, understandably had quite the rivalry. There used to be a cutout of a wooden sailboat on the Yacht Club at Cory – that was apparently taken from Camp Iroquois. A metal sheriff-type badge used to hang on the crossbeam of cabin M-4 at Camp Cory – *that* was apparently taken from Camp Iroquois. There was at one time an Indian head scowling from atop the upstairs entrance to the Junior Boathouse – that was taken from Camp Iroquois. This latter piece of décor was the subject of several rescue attempts on the part of Camp Iroquois in the 1990s and 2000s; they did not know that the head had been destroyed for some time.

In 2000 the Camp Director of Iroquois called Cory and informed us that several of his staff members would be attempting to steal our K-boats that night. I, Leadership Director Dave Ghidiu, kitchen staff Ben Goossen, and possibly some others, dressed in black and waited on the hill overlooking the Y-dock, on a stakeout. The Camp Iroquois boat came, but quickly sped away when it realized that we were ready (they realized this because we were in the process of responding to a prank when they arrived).

Soon thereafter, possibly in 2001 or 2002, Camp Iroquois once again tried to perform a nighttime prank. Their boat, though, got its propellers caught in the peppermint lines of our swimming area. They called for a rescue boat. That boat's propellers got caught, too. The third boat started to tow the other two back to Iroquois, but its engine overheated and broke down halfway back. Finally, the fourth boat managed to rescue the other three.

In 2008-2009 the Camp Iroquois situation came to a head, as can be seen by the incidents related above. If all of the encounters with the camp over these two summers (or longer) are taken together, then relations with this camp could be classified as a long-term, "creeping crisis." They accused us of stealing some water jug while they were on one of their hikes, which of course we did not do. Around 2003 we generally stopped pranking Camp Iroquois, instead focusing on running a good camp ourselves. Even the pranks of the late 1990s and early 2000s were, on our part, miniscule.

In 2009 we began documenting every incident with Camp Iroquois, and started taking pictures of them if they came too close to camp (this happened once or twice, to my knowledge). We talked to the CEO of the Rochester YMCA, and eventually to the Yates County Sheriff's Department, who warned off Camp Iroquois.

They are, in all, a juvenile camp. There have been a few incidents since then, sometimes involving the theft of the Camp Cory sign, taunting, or throwing rocks. The creeping crisis, apparently, continues.

Chapter 3:

The Interlopers of 2000

I was a CIT in 2000, and Dave Ghidiu was my
Leadership Director. There were eight of us in the
group: four guys and four girls. All of the other
campers had to be in bed and quiet by 10 pm (at least
in theory) but we were allowed to have the Senior
Upper Athletic Field all to ourselves from 10 pm until
midnight, every night. Also, in those days, we didn't
have a counselor supervising us. All that was required

52

of us was that we be quiet enough so as not to disturb the rest of camp, and that we get ourselves ready for bed by midnight.

One night, we had been laying out in the field, talking about something philosophical I'm sure, and I was walking over to the bathroom to brush my teeth. There was a line of trees along the eastern end of the athletic field, blocking us off from East Lake Road. But in the southeast corner of the field was a bare spot, and I looked up there on my way over to the bathroom, and I thought maybe I saw a person standing there.

I brushed my teeth and headed back to our row of four little cabins. The cabins aren't there anymore; they were replaced with a big, 32-bed all-season building in 2005. We were all standing around outside our cabins, talking before we went to bed, and a counselor from Walmsley came up to talk to us. He asked us if we had been hollering, and we honestly had been very quiet that night. CIT Heather asked, "Howling? You're asking if we were howling?" And I'm still not sure if she was serious or not. We assured the counselor that we hadn't been making any noise, and then he left. A few minutes later we said goodnight to one another, and our two counselors, Kevin and Caitlin, came up the hill to go to bed, too.

Rob and I lived in a cabin with Dave, but Dave was a Central Staff member, so he had night security patrol ("Claw duty") some nights, and that summer he also ran the camp store, so he was very rarely there by midnight. Rob and I were in our cabin, CIT-3 (pron. "sit three"), and Kevin headed past our door on his way to CIT-4. There was a small hole in the sliding green wooden door, and Kevin poked a couple of fingers through while saying goodnight. Rob and I stroked his fingers while saying goodnight back, and then we heard someone shouting from the middle of the athletic field. I have no idea what he was saying, but it was something like, "Bluh, bluh, bluh... Boo-lah!" Rob asked, "What was that?" And Kevin agitatedly replied, "I don't know. I'm scared!" But he was also sort of joking. I could hear the rest of the CITs start to freak out, and then a couple seconds later Dave came bolting up the hill, shouting, "Everyone get in the same cabin! Everyone in CIT-1, everyone in CIT-1!" We ran out the door and all eight of us barricaded ourselves in the first cabin, which belonged to a couple of the girls, Heather and Leah.

Caitlin watched us while a bunch of the other staff members around camp chased the interlopers around. We heard voices shouting from all over camp at one time or another, and once or twice a car pulled into camp and then sped away. The girls were all pretty scared, as was CIT James. Before we had left our cabin, I had grabbed a real guitar – albeit stringless – that I had found in the drama supplies a few days earlier. I was holding it by the neck, ready to swing, in case anyone tried to come through the door.

A few minutes into being trapped in the cabin ("No offense Caitlin, but you being our guard doesn't really make us feel safe") Rob took the guitar away from me to use himself. I needed some kind of weapon, I determined, so I took a broom from next to the door, took a Mag light, and then took some duct tape and taped the Mag light to the end of the broom, making a sort of sight for my weapon. So Rob and I were standing there with very creative, very impractical weapons.

At one point we decided that there might be someone behind the cabin, or maybe underneath. So Caitlin took her flashlight and walked a circle around the cabin while Rob and I were standing next to the door with our weapons at the ready. Heather was crying that she wanted to go home – she had wanted to go home a lot, especially when they had taken away her cell phone, which she wasn't supposed to have anyway. No one had cell phones back then, especially

not campers, and cell phones didn't really work on

camp grounds anyway. But the whole time, while Rob

and I were playing the hero, and James and the girls

were crying and getting scared, Aaron was lying on

one of the beds, calling to us that the interlopers were

gone, and he just wanted to sleep. He was being

annoyed, and funny. By this time we had gotten used

to his sense of humor. It was a dry wit.

Caitlin came back; she opened the door to see

Rob and me standing there, weapons raised. And after

a while Dave and Kevin came back up the hill.

Apparently they had chased some kids all

around camp. At one point the Walmsley counselor

who had come to talk to us earlier in the night was

chasing one of them across a bridge and was mere

inches away from grabbing the kid's shirt. They had a

car, maybe parked up by the road, and they had pulled

into camp to try to turn around, or possibly to pick up

some of their comrades. After they pulled out of camp, Dave told the rest of the counselors who protected camp that night, "If they pull back in, close the gate behind them, and then break their windshield." The counselors were, after all, armed with baseball bats and the like.

It turns out that a girl in our group had a boyfriend who was on his high school's baseball team, and they had been in Penn Yan to play that night. He was a jackass, and he didn't see any problem with sneaking onto a camp to see his girlfriend. So the interlopers were him and a few of his friends. We found this out maybe a month later, after a few of us had been hired back.

***

COMMENTARY:

This was perhaps the first camp emergency I had to deal with when in a staff (or semi-staff) capacity. The counselors, especially Kevin and Dave, did not necessarily remain entirely calm, but it

nevertheless appears they reacted in a proper manner.

When we first heard the shouting in the middle of the

field, Kevin still maintained a sense of humor, saying

"I'm scared," in a comical tone.

Dave quickly realized that our vulnerability was

in our separateness, and adjusted to get all eight of us

in one place. By consolidating us like this it was

easier to guard us, easier to keep track of us, and

easier to make sure, at all times, that all eight of us

remained safe. (I replicated this action somewhat

when reacting to the "Missing" Walmsley Campers of

2004 and The Interloping Boater of 2003 – see *infra*).

It would have been very easy for a gung-ho

Counselor or Leadership Director to immediately focus

on chasing and capturing the interlopers. Young,

stupid, college-aged kids (especially males) crave

adventure and excitement. Luckily, Dave realized

that securing the campers took first priority. Only

after that was accomplished was he free to give chase.

It would have been far better to allow the interlopers

to go free (as he did) and keep us safe, than to

successfully capture the interlopers while

compromising our safety. Just as when coming upon a

purse-snatching assailant who has just knocked a

victim over into a busy street: saving the victim takes

precedence over retrieving the purse and capturing the

assailant.

While we CITs waited in the cabin, most of us

were terribly afraid. Aaron's humor was good for us.

It helped to keep us calm.

Chapter 4

Code Reds and Code Blues

Lost Camper Procedures – Waterfront "Code Red"

All staff should be familiar and comfortable with the

following procedures:

Upon determining that a swimmer is unaccounted for:

1. The staff member at the buddy board checks out

    all remaining campers.

2. One designated counselor radios or reports to

    the program office to announce the missing

camper's name over the PA system and for all other available staff to report to the appropriate waterfront **immediately**. (The PA message will be "*Attention all staff, attention all staff, Code Red at __________ waterfront.*")

3. One counselor, preferably the camper's swimming instructor, goes to the village to try to locate him or her.

4. One staff member shall remain in each village to supervise the campers. All available staff and lifeguards assemble in the intermediate and swimmers areas – at the direction of the Waterfront Director – in a straight line at arm's length apart from each other. A few swimmers will sweep the beginners area:

    a. The team proceeds out from shore, searching with foot sweeps until reaching chest deep water

b. At this point, all swimmers dive on command and search the bottom with open eyes and groping hands for a distance of 2 body lengths and then surface

c. The line then straightens, backs up three feet [to the farthest-back staff member], and dives again on command. The Waterfront Director or line leader will initiate these commands.

5. The Frog Squad members will search their assigned areas.

6. Step 4 is repeated until the end of the swimming area is reached. If the swimmer has not yet been located, the team works back to shore in the same manner as in 4b and 4c.

7. The search is continued until:

a. The body is found

b. The swimmer is located elsewhere in

camp

c. Proper authorities take over the

investigation

Lost Camper Procedure – Land "Code Blue"

1. When a camper is determined to be missing
    during a routine head check or attendance, a
    counselor should report to the office/radio the
    office where the Executive Director or Associate
    Executive Director will initiate the Missing
    Camper Procedure.

2. The Executive Director or Associate Executive
    Director will notify the Sheriff as needed. The
    Office Manager will go to the road to greet the
    Sheriff. The Associate Executive Director will
    send a runner to the infirmary to inform the
    nurse and verify that the missing camper is not
    in the infirmary. A staff member then
    announces over the PA *"This is a CODE BLUE,
    Jane Smith please report to the office
    immediately."*

3. When staff hear the announcement made they are to immediately have all children sit where they are and begin asking each camper if they are Jane Smith. When campers are at their activity areas the Chief will coordinate this, when with their villages the Village Head will coordinate this. All staff [who] are not assigned to a village or activity area should report to the office to be delegated as needed. This includes kitchen staff, maintenance staff, the Program Directors, the Leadership Director, and any off-duty staff. Initially these staff will be used to search areas outside of camp, including the road and the nearby golf course.

4. Each activity area or village is responsible for searching adjacent buildings and grounds. The Chief or Village Head will delegate staff to search these areas. See attached sheet for a list

of the areas assigned to each program area/village.

5. Once the designated areas are searched, a runner should be sent to the office to indicate that the specific area is clear. These runners will then be used in other capacities.

6. The Associate Executive Director will contact the Sheriff when warranted. The Associate Executive Director or Executive Director will contact the parents if necessary.

Missing Camper Procedure—Nighttime

1. If a camper is discovered missing from bed during Claw bed checks, the person on claw will wake the counselor and verify that the camper is not in the cabin, in the infirmary, or on an off-camp trip.

2. After verifying that the camper is not in the cabin or bathroom the person on Claw will wake

the Associate Executive Director. The Associate

Executive Director will wake other staff to aid

in the search.

3. The Associate Executive Director will contact

the Sheriff when warranted.

4. The Associate Executive Director or Executive

Director will contact the parents if necessary.

<u>Lost Camper Procedures – Search Areas</u>

If a camper is missing during activity time:

Archery

Junior Athletic Field, Whispering Pines Showerhouse,
Staff Lounge

Arts and Crafts

Junior boathouse

Aquatics

Junior Waterfront

Athletics

Senior Village Bathrooms

Canoeing and Kayaking | Outdoor Education
Senior Boathouse, Chapel, Wells Fire Circle

High Ropes
J-1 through J-9, High Ropes Course, Alumni Cabin

Sailing
M-2 through M-5, Maijgren Bathrooms, Sailing
Waterfront

Office Staff
S-1 through S-13

Kitchen Staff
Dining Hall, Dining Hall Bathrooms

Remember:

- At least one staff member must stay in each

  activity area; the Village Head or Chief

  designates this person.

- ☐ Keep all radios clear unless pertinent to the emergency

- ☐ All activities must stop immediately during a Code Blue

- ☐ Every counselor searching should be constantly calling the missing camper's name

- ☐ When the camper is found, send a runner to the office immediately and report with the child

Lost Camper Procedures – Search Areas

If a camper is missing during village time:

Craig Village

All CAbins, Junior Bathroom, Junior Waterfront, Ropes Course, Arts & Crafts, Archery

Wells Village

All Cabins, Senior Bathroom/Shower, Chapel, Wells Fire Circle, Senior Boathouse

Walmsley Village

All Cabins, Maijgren Bathroom

Maijgren Village

All Cabins, Yacht Club, Beach from Senior Boathouse to Ski-Dock, All Boats on the Water

Leadership Village

Lodge, Upper Athletic Field, Central Area
Remember:

- At least one staff member must stay in each activity area; the Village Head or Chief designates this person.

- Keep all radios clear unless pertinent to the emergency

- All activities must stop immediately during a Code Blue

- Every counselor searching should be constantly calling the missing camper's name

▪ When the camper is found, send a runner to the office immediately and report with the child

***

Commentary:

I know of no other camp that has a waterfront emergency system like the Code Red. It was apparently begun by Jerry Elliott when he became Camp Director in 1975. He came from a waterfront background, and thought it best to make his staff experts when it came to water rescue and emergencies – an especially prudent choice given the expanse of Cory's waterfront area and activities. Apparently, during staff training Jerry and his Waterfront Director would have the entire staff stand in a circle in the water, facing one another, with their eyes closed. He and the Waterfront Director would swim around the circle, splashing certain counselors, and taking some of them under so that they could practice escapes.

Lifeguarding, especially Red Cross lifeguarding, has been dumbed-down over the years. For example, lifeguard instructions manuals used to contain an entire chapter on escapes. More recent manuals contain a short section.

The "immediately" language when paging someone to the waterfront began in 2002. The director that year imported much of his vernacular from Camp Seagull in North Carolina. Most non-emergency pages over the P.A. system ended with "at this time" (e.g., "Samuel Moulthrop, please report to the office at this time"). Medical emergencies ended with "now." This code meant that a counselor and the Camp Nurse or EMT should drop whatever they were doing and run. In the event of thunderstorms, staff and campers were told to "hustle, hustle, hustle" to their cabins, or to the nearest shelter. And for Code Reds and Code Blues, the word "immediately" was used ("Code Red" as a term was temporarily retired for that summer).

The Code Red, and its land-based counterpart, the Code Blue, are well-practiced. Ideally, a Code Red drill is carried out nearly a dozen times during staff training, and at least once a week for the remainder of the summer. Because the drills are so well-practiced, staff responses to them are intended to be largely automatic. Very little direction actually takes place during the response to the emergency. Again, this is a prudent thing to do at a camp with so much waterfront space. Because the emergency is not a surprise, there is no need for contraction of authority (where the highest leader necessarily makes decisions) or innovative ideas (which would be generated in a long-term surprise scenario).

Emergencies may generally be split into four different categories:

I.   No Surprise, Long Term

II.   Surprise, Long Term

III.   No Surprise, Short Term

IV.   Surprise, Short Term

(*see* Charles F. Hermann, "Threat, Time, and Surprise:
A Simulation of International Crisis," in Charles F.
Hermann, ed., *International Crises: Insights from
Behavioral Research.* New York: Free Press, 1972).

Code Reds and Code Blues, Type III crises, have
a prescripted response of every participant following
standard operating procedure:

III. No Surprise, Short Term

Everyone follows standard operating procedure

But one of the problems I noticed is that Code
Reds were generally practiced only at the swimming
waterfront – not at the boating or sailing waterfronts.
That meant that, should an emergency at the sailing
waterfront have occurred, there was no "standard
operating procedure" to follow. When I held a drill

75

with the "frog squad" at the sailing waterfront, participants afterwards were interested in setting a standard operating procedure for the future. This would have been a bad idea unless we were planning on drilling the sailing waterfront Code Red with some regularity.

Otherwise, if an emergency had occurred and everyone were expected to follow standard operating procedures, much time would have been spent trying to remember these procedures. Because the boating Code Red was a different type of emergency, a different response was called for:

IV. Surprise, Short Term

Contraction of authority

Quick decision-making by the highest leader

Essentially, the Waterfront Director, Sailing Master, or the highest ranked person on scene would direct the rest of the staff. The rest of the staff, in turn, would follow these orders. As a benefit, this way it is likely that the person with the most emergency response experience is the one making decisions. The nighttime Code Blue is a good example, too, of a Type IV emergency. It would be impracticable to drill it, so the Associate Executive Director (Camp Director) makes unquestioned decisions. Shortly after the publication of the digital version of this book, the Central Staff had occasion to respond to a missing camper at nighttime emergency. The highest ranked person available at the time split the Central Staff into pairs and designated a sector for each pair to search, while calling out the name of the missing campers (it ended up being a prank, and all of the campers were found without incident).

Back to waterfront emergencies: of course, if we had chosen to, we could have conducted weekly drills of the boating emergency, in which case it would have become a Type III emergency and standard operating procedures would have made more sense.

Similarly, I once saw a staff member attempt a lifeguard rescue of another staff member by allowing her to catch her breath and then swimming in to shore with her. This would not do: I told him, "If she needs to be rescued, you should actually perform the rescue." So he did.

Lifeguard rescue maneuvers are drilled – they should be followed because they are practiced and are what will come more naturally to the rescuer. He would be calmer performing them, and would react better to unforeseen circumstances (e.g. having to perform an escape).

When emergencies are likely to occur, they should be practiced frequently. That avoids the surprise when they do happen.

79

Chapter 5:

The Triple K-Boat Capsize of 2005

Saturday, 30 July 2005. We have had some very heavy-wind days this week. On one of them, we dealt with a capsized K-boat, skippered by C.S., during morning activities. She capsized K-boats twice more in the afternoon. Tuesday night Dave, Alex, and I met with [Program Director] Bonnie Rowe to discuss C.S. She has now been placed in Arts & Crafts. Though they interrupt normal sailing, I do enjoy taking part in on-water rescues.

I was the Maijgren Village Head this summer, and therefore supervised all campers in the specialized sailing program. As a camper, I had been in a capsized sailboat – it had been at once a terrifying and unreal experience. I then drifted too close to the propellers of the pontoon rescue boat, and a counselor in the water with me had to pull me away at the last second.

For those who aren't familiar with them, K-boats are 16-foot two-sail boats named for the Kohinoor diamond. They are huge, heavy fiberglass tubs – durable and steady, but not terribly fast. Originally made of wood, they were built out of fiberglass beginning around the 1970s. They only capsize in terrible weather (or when handled by a completely incompetent sailor) and are therefore great boats on which to learn to sail. At one time Camp Cory had what was apparently the largest fleet of K's in the world, though by 2014 the only one that remained at camp was repurposed as a flower planter up near the camp entrance. This is not necessarily such a bad thing, since the K-boats had some definite problems. For one thing, they were not used by any other yacht club in the area – that distinction goes to the International 420. For another thing, K-boats are simply not *meant* to capsize. And once they do, they cannot sail until they are towed in, beached, and bailed out.

The morning in question was a particularly windy one. There had been several on-water issues so far over the summer, but a K-boat had yet to capsize (sometimes whole summers would go by without a boat capsizing). And then it happened. Sailing Master Dave Ghidiu and I headed out on the pontoon boat to rescue the capsized boat. We saw the counselor at the boat with all of the campers. They had seemingly followed the capsize procedures (which were a written policy in the sailing village, but which were not regularly drilled). The counselor began to justify herself: "Water just started *pouring* in-" but Dave and I cut her off.

We got the kids out of the water, righted the boat (which was now partially submerged) and towed it in. The counselor, I believe, had to stay on the sailboat in order to keep it pointed at our stern – this prevented the rope from breaking. I may have also performed this steering, at least at some point during the day.

We got the boat to shore and bailed it out as best we could. That afternoon, the very same counselor capsized a boat with campers again. Dave and I followed a similar procedure as in the morning, although we had some of the kinks worked out already (e.g., having someone on the K-boat in order to steer it straight). We began bailing that boat out. By this time, the original boat was ready to be sailed again.

And apparently it was ready to be capsized again, too.
The same counselor capsized the boat. By that time,
Dave and I didn't even get excited and I felt like I
knew exactly what to do. We were used to it.

At the end of the summer, counselors who have
done particularly stupid things often receive a Silver
Spike Award – a nail sticking through a block of wood.
That summer, this particular counselor received a
block with three nails.

***

Commentary:

There is a reason why I placed this crisis at
number 5 – approximately halfway through the book.
This crisis helps to explain the epigram at the
beginning of this work, and also contains the thesis of
this work: the best way to respond well to emergencies
is to have already responded to many emergencies.

This is why in surprising, short-term
emergencies (Type IV), it is best to have a contraction

84

of authority with quick decision-making by the highest

leader. That person, in theory, is someone with lots of

experience. That person has practiced the drills

before. That person has heard of, thought of, (read of),

or even enacted creative ideas in Type II crises (*see*

Chapter 9). So when a Type IV crisis comes along,

that leader is hopefully able to think and act quickly.

In short, when responding to emergencies, the highest

decision-maker should be calmer than others, and

should have a bigger arsenal of potential responses

from which to immediately draw.

Chapter 6

This is the crisis detailed somewhat in the introduction to this work. To review, on a beautiful summer day, one of the largest villages in the camp had gone on a lunchtime canoe trip. On the way back, the Village Head radioed to the office that he was missing two campers, and had no idea where they were.

I headed out on the ski boat with the Program Director and the Waterskiing Chief. At first we did not know what to do. We didn't even know which two campers were missing. No counselor could seem to think of anyone in particular who was gone, but the Village Head swore that, according to his numbers, he was two campers short.

As his village was beginning to land at the Senior Boathouse, Program Director Chris Dudley and I somehow decided that I would be dropped off at the boathouse and coordinate things there. I could not wrap my head around the incongruity, and eventually determined that someone, potentially one of the village's counselors, had to have been wrong, and was actually missing two campers he had just forgotten about, or whom he had not gotten the time to know.

But the boathouse was chaos. The village was also somewhat late coming back, so not only were all of those campers there, but all of the campers who had canoeing and kayaking class in the beginning of the afternoon were beginning to show up. There seemed to be no way to get a clear, reliable count of all of the campers in a calm, rational manner.

I had someone help me get hockey sticks or some other straight items and laid them down on the floor of the boathouse stage. I then separated the stage into sections. Each section represented a cabin in the village. I had all of the campers sit in their designated spaces, I believe with their counselors, and had everyone begin looking around to see if they noticed anyone missing. I hoped that, given enough people looking at all of the campers present from their own cabins, *some*one would finally notice a glaring deficiency.

My plan was cut short, but my next step would have been to call the office and ask them to read off names of each person in each cabin, while I had everyone sitting in his or her own cabin's separate area. This would, once and for all, ensure who was actually missing. And it would be easier to do than having everyone milling about, because campers were all in logical physical categories and spaces.

I got a radio call – the crisis was over, and I was to release everyone to go to his or her next activity. I do not believe I knew, at first, why this was.

***

COMMENTARY:

No one drowned, as I may have feared at the time. The reason for the crisis was much more banal: the Village Head simply forgot about two campers who had already gone home already earlier in the week. They had left on the first or second day of the session, and it appears he actually did update his master list (otherwise there would have been many previous opportunities to notice two missing girls). But for this trip, later in the week, perhaps he printed out a new attendance sheet based off of the original Sunday check-in document – a file that still contained the names of these two girls. Before heading out on the trip, he had memorized the number of campers he was supposed to have, but did not necessarily do a head count of the entire village until returning on the water.

I got the idea of separating the campers out by cabin, I think, from our fire drill procedure (and also from a similar 2003 crisis, *infra*). The New York State Department of Health mandates that the camp perform a fire drill once a week, and the American Camps Association likes to see that we keep track of our response times. During these fire drills, cabins hustle up to a pre-designated field, on the edge of camp. Each counselor counts his or her campers, and reports to a Village Head. A Village Head reports to the office once his or her entire village is accounted for. The drill ends when all villages are accounted for. (Usually the communication with the office is done *via* radio, but once or twice a summer I had non-radio drills, so we could replicate what it would actually be like to send a runner in case radio use were precluded for some reason).

I think the separation of campers into cabins was a good idea. It brought much needed sanity to the situation, and made the entire village (of nearly 50 children and counselors, I believe) participants in the problem. As Linus's Law says: "given enough eyeballs, all bugs are shallow."

What this means in the computer programming context is, given a large enough beta-tester and co-developer base, almost any problem will be characterized quickly and the fix will be obvious to *some*one (*see* Eric S. Raymond. *The Cathedral & The Bazaar*. Sebastopel: O'Reilly, 2001, 30). This applies to the situation presented here in a general way: with all campers and counselors actually looking and noticing their cabin groups – with which they were hopefully familiar – it was less likely that one careless counselor's mistake could go unnoticed.

Linus's Law also can apply on a much larger scale to the summer camp (or organization) in general. The more people who are exposed to emergency situations, the more people will have larger "arsenals" of responses (*see* Chapter 5). And the more people with large arsenals, the greater the likelihood that creative, successful solutions will come about in the case of a Type II emergency (*see* Chapter 9).

Chapter 7:

The Interloping Boater of 2003

It was dinnertime and a storm had been

brewing all afternoon – we may have even called

thunder warnings once or twice during afternoon

activities. But now the entire camp was gathered in

the Dining Hall. Most of the Village Heads were on

their night off, so several members of my generation

were acting village heads for the evening – I was Acting Walmsley Village Head and therefore supervised a large village of teenaged campers.

I was walking through Central Area on some errand when a man stopped me. This was before Day Camp existed, so visitors to camp were more rare in those days. He was an older gentleman with a seersucker-type suit and either a barbershop quartet hat or a fedora. He walked with a halting, herky-jerky gait. The man asked me if I had a light, and I said no. I later learned that he had a motorboat docked down at the Y-Dock. I headed back into the Dining Hall and, I believe, informed someone higher up in the chain of command that the man was there.

Apparently he had asked at least one other person for a light, too. After dinner, several of us on staff learned that the man had gone into his boat down at the Y-Dock and had driven away. Someone claimed that there had been a young girl on the boat with him, and no one knew whether she was one of our campers or not.

There being the possibility that one of our campers had just been kidnapped, the next task was to confirm or disconfirm it. Sailing Master Jared Engel took the Party Boat and began chasing after the man's boat. By now it was time for the campers to go to the Camp Store, and there was no practicable way to get a good head count to make sure all campers were present. Similar to the situation I would have the following summer, what needed to be done here was a quick attendance call of the entire camp, but without the potential for causing panic.

I decided that we should call a thunder warning, even though no thunder had been heard. That would cause all of the campers in camp to go back ("hustle, hustle, hustle") to their cabins. Then, Village Heads could walk around and make sure all of their campers were accounted for. The plan was executed.

All campers were accounted for. Though Jared Engel lost the interloping boater, it became clear that the girl on the boat was actually his daughter, or at least was not involved in camp in any way. I called the real Walmsley Village Head to update her on the situation so she would not be surprised when she got back from her night off. Why the interloping boater chose to dock at Camp Cory that day remains a mystery.

***

Commentary:

This was a pretty typical Type IV crisis. The only thing that really made it atypical was that there was not an ideal "highest leader" present to make all of the decisions. Jared, who probably would have been the person to make the decisions in the absence of some of the other Central Staff, had not wrongly taken the initiative to chase down the interloping boater. We were lucky in this case, I believe, that the other staff members present (i.e., the other Acting Village Heads) recognized the desirability of my faux-thunderstorm idea. The outcome could have easily gone another way: another inexperienced leader could have had what he or she thought was a good idea, and with no experienced person present, that bad idea could have been executed.

Although we succeeded in avoiding panic and in ensuring the general safety and welfare of the camp, this crisis is in a way a good lesson in what not to do. In later years (the late 2000s, in particular), staff members were given an organizational chart, a "staff hierarchy," in their staff manuals. When the chart was explained during staff training week, the Camp Director would explicitly tell everyone the chain of command. He would explain that when he was gone, the Program Directors were in charge. When they were gone, the Leadership Director was in charge, and so on. This left no question in anyone's mind about who the "highest leader" would be.

In the early 2000s, when the directors were absent from the camp, there was no set plan in place determining who was in charge — authority devolved separately upon the four or five village heads. In 2003, I do not believe we had a consensus on who the highest leader was at camp on that particular evening. The previous summer had seen some changes in the personnel structuring at camp. In 2001, too, there had been drastic restructuring, with a very young Assistant Director, and a relatively-powerful upper-tier of the Central Staff that was referred to derogatorily as the "big five" (the Junior Village Director, the "Senior Village Director," the Program Director/Leadership Director, the Assistant Director, and the Executive Director). In 2002, Mark Dibble was hired as a year-round "Program Director" whose title changed to "Camp Director" during the summer.

There was also a seasonal "Program Director," Chris Dudley, whose job was somewhat equivalent to the late-2000s/early 2010s Program Director, although some of his responsibilities were handled by the Camp Director. In short, the staff hierarchy was not as clear as it could have been, or as clear as it has been in more recent years.

The crisis was resolved (in fact, never blossoming into a full-blown crisis), but it would have been better if we had had one person, or maybe two, we *knew* to be in charge of the camp in the absence of the directors and village heads.

Chapter 8:

"The Great Wind Blast of Aught-4"

It was during the middle of one of the activity

periods down at the Junior Waterfront that the Sailing

Chief, Alex Baum, called out over the radio that he

spotted a wall of rain and storm moving north up the

lake. We at the Waterfront began checking all of the

kids out of the water – both because we knew the

storm was coming, and because I knew I'd want to

send staff members to other areas to help with the

soon-to-be-arrived crisis. I couldn't send lifeguards away if I still had kids in the water.

Alex kept calling out how close the wall of the storm was. First it was a little south of Keuka College, within sight of camp. Then he said that the wall of rain had reached Keuka College. Next, the college itself was no longer visible. He had begun sending all of his boats in, but we could tell that there was no way they would all get to shore before the storm hit.

Alex's countdown reached its final stages — based on the speed of the approaching storm, he was able to predict almost to the second when it would hit. My swimmers were now all out of the water and had taken shelter in the Junior Boathouse. From our vantage point at the end of the dock, Walmsley Village Head Patrick Foster and I could see the six or eight sailboats that remained on the water. The grey tumult approached from the south, blotting out everything. The wall of the tempest drove up across the lake. Every sailboat it hit, with only one exception, capsized or was torn asunder. The huge J-24 broke apart. K-boats and JY-15s flipped, some turtling. One boat remained upright, because its skipper had wisely lowered his sails before the wind blast hit.

Pat and I still had our lifeguard tubes strapped across our chests. He called out to me, "We've got boats over" and he started running down the beach towards the sailing waterfront. I followed, running, and we turned right into the water. I kept my knees high, as trained, so that the viscosity of the water wouldn't trip me. Once the water became deep enough, Pat and I leapt forward and began swimming, trailing our tubes behind us.

There were some boats that had capsized almost inside the cove of the sailing waterfront – I swam to one of those first to prevent it from turtling. Once a boat turtled that close to shore, its mast often became stuck in the muck, and could not then be righted

without assist of motor.

Pat and I righted some boats, and I then rode

out farther into the lake with the Party Boat, or

perhaps with a different rescue boat. A counselor was

at the J-24 with a wrench, working on putting it back

together so it could be sailed in.

The storm had essentially been just one big

blast of wind. As soon as it passed, the skies cleared,

though the damage it had levied remained.

***

Commentary:

We were lucky that the Sailing Chief had been

able to notify us of the oncoming storm. By evacuating

the waterfront, we had been able to make more

rescuers available sooner.

I looked back on this crisis years later, when I

was debriefing the backboarding incident (*see* Chapter

1). Here, Pat and I had run down the beach to rescue

the boats, much as two staff members did during the backboarding incident. In neither case was running necessary; in either case it could have resulted in further injury to one of the runners. As mentioned before: there is almost no reason to run. The few seconds we saved by doing so were not more valuable than safety and relative calmness.

Once we were on the water after the windblast, Pat and I took the initiative to right some of the boats that were in the cove. But after that, Sailing Chief Alex Baum and Maijgren Village Head/Sailing Master Dave Ghidiu – the highest leaders present, and the ones with the most expertise on sailboat-related crises – directed our actions, and ferried us around the lake to where we were needed.

I don't know what was going through the head of Counselor Evan Engel, who lowered his sails before the wind blast hit, but it would seem he absolutely did the right thing. Had he been able to get to shore in time, that would have been the best thing to do. But if

he hadn't been able to make it, or even if the outcome

was questionable, lowering his sails before the wind

hit saved his boat from capsizing. The wind blast had

nothing on which to find purchase. He, it would seem,

did not panic.

Possibly the best thing any of the sailors could

have done would have been to sail towards shore, and

only upon realizing that he or she would not make it,

to lower his or her sails. With everyone sailing towards

shore, several boats ended up capsizing right near the

beach, where the water was shallow. As a result, one

or two boats' masts became stuck in the muck at the

bottom of the lake. Given the resources required to

right a boat in that condition, it almost would have

been better for them to have stayed out in the middle

of the lake.

Chapter 9:

The High Ropes Hair Entanglement

I was in the program office on a typical sunny afternoon when I got the call that there was an emergency at the high ropes course. There was a girl stuck at the top of the challenge course with her hair tangled into the bracket of her belaying equipment. On my way out of the office, I paused to grab a pair of sharp scissors.

When I got to the high ropes course, I saw the girl standing on top of the challenge course, thirty feet in the air. The High Ropes Chief was there, and eventually the Camp Director, the other Program Director, and several visitors arrived.

The problem was that the girl's hair was running, along with the climbing rope, through her bracket. The more she lowered, the more the rope went through one end of the bracket, and the more it pulled her hair straight through. The young girl at the top of the challenge course was starting to panic, and the High Ropes Chief was either nervous or was panicking herself. Myself and the other Central Staff started making light of the situation.

One of the other persons present saw immediately what needed to be done: we on the ground would have to pull in the rope *a la* an Australian Belay. In normal belaying, one person on the ground pulls the rope as the climber climbs. The rope goes through a bracket and is held safely in place by friction. In the so-called Australian Belay, several persons on the ground hold the rope as the climber climbs, and they all pull like in a tug of war. The safety of the climber is ensured by the sheer number and combined strength of the crowd pulling on the ground.

We continued to take a joking attitude, called over to the dishboy cabin, which was located nearby, and enlisted some of the kitchen staff to help us all pull the rope. A few visitors were still there, merely observing. One of them commented sarcastically, "I'm glad this is all so funny." Her tone led me to believe that, in her opinion, we should all have been taking it much more seriously.

As we pulled the rope on the ground, the High Ropes Chief and the girl victim up in the air were able to have more slack in the rope. When that happened, they could work the rope back through the bracket, backwards, and the rope brought the girl's hair back with it. Once the girl's hair was out, she was able to rappel down to the ground and go on to her next activity, or perhaps back to her cabin. The scissors that I had brought were not needed.

***

Commentary:

This is a good example of a Type II emergency or crisis, where there is surprise, but there is a long time in which to react.

II. Surprise, Long Term

Innovative Ideas are Generated

A couple years earlier I had heard of a similar thing happening at camp in the early morning (while the High Ropes Chief was setting up the climbing wall). The solution then had been to use shears to cut parts of the victim's hair off. This was why I had grabbed the scissors from the Program Office. They ended up not being necessary, but I think they help to illustrate that experience, even second-hand experience gleaned through listening to others' stories, can lead to the immediate planning and proposal of possible solutions to a problem. A less experienced staff member would not have known that scissors might be necessary, and would therefore not have even thought to bring them. Precious minutes might have been lost in the event that the situation called for the cutting of hair.

The sense of humor was absolutely important in the situation. The visitor, with her sarcastic comment, was absolutely wrong. The victim was panicking. Even the High Ropes Chief seemed rattled. We on the ground, in complete safety, had a responsibility to project an attitude that everything was going to be all right. Apart from the potential impact on morale, a panicked staff member or camper might have had a more difficult time with the maneuver they would eventually be called on to do.

Young, inexperienced staff members have a greater tendency to panic. I remember another occasion, when several of the Central Staff members were celebrating the end of the week with some pizza in the Camp Office building. A panicked young counselor ran onto the back porch and into the office where we were all sitting. She struggled to communicate through her emotion, eventually telling us that someone had fallen down by the water and was injured, not able to get back up. The counselor's attitude was actually somewhat humorous, since it was clear from her description that the person who had fallen was in no immediate danger.

The Camp Director adopted a humorous attitude, asking inane and stupid questions as if he didn't understand. *Who* fell? *Where*? Wait, one more question… *who* fell? The panicking staff member may have started to become frustrated, but we all followed the Camp Director's suit — one of us took a huge bit of pizza, chewed a couple of times, then pointed at the panicking staff member quizzically, "…Where is she?" I hope the lesson was not lost on the panicking staff member, although I fear it might have been. Excited young persons running around the camp at night looking for an injured person would have been no way to respond to an emergency.

In both the high ropes hair entanglement situation and in the fallen staff member situation, the crisis was unexpected, but there was no short-term emergency. The girl with the tangled hair could have theoretically waited on top of the challenge course for hours. The fallen staff member could have lain on the ground (hopefully with a blanket) for hours, as well, if necessary. There was no need to centralize authority. There was not necessarily an established procedure to follow (although hair getting stuck in climbing equipment is rather common, so a good activity coordinator should know what to do). In both cases, there was time to brainstorm; there was time to figure out the best course of action before acting. Innovative ideas had the potential to be generated. With regard to the fallen person, there was time to be calm and consider our options. With regard to the hair entanglement, my proposal involved cutting hair. But a better idea was the Australian Belay to relieve slack in the rope.

Chapter 10:

The Runaway C.I.T. of 2010

August 16th 2010 (taken from an incident report)

I was watching two day campers at the pavilion when I saw a person walking up to the road, towards the sign. I wasn't sure who it was, and I was the only person watching the kids, so I radioed Pat. He said that the person was S.G., the CIT. Pat and Blake then came over from Craig and began running up to the road after Sarah.

I went into the Dining Hall and got someone to watch the day campers. I began running, but then walked over to the camp van, picked up Blake, and drove up to the road. S.G. was already several hundred yards away from camp, going towards town. Pat was chasing after her. I pulled the van into a driveway, let Blake out [in front of S.G.], and Blake and Pat began talking to S.G. I called Mark, who said we should just let her call her parents [to pick her up] because we had better things to deal with, and she was a CIT. After a few minutes, S.G. agreed to come back to camp.

I pulled the van into a driveway farther down the road, picked everyone up, and brought them back to camp. S.G. waited in the office, then packed her things during cabin level, and waited in the office some more until her father picked her up.

***

Commentary:

By this time, my final summer at Camp Cory, my philosophy of crisis response had been pretty well solidified. I had seen disasters aplenty, and had already written up the reports from the backboarding incident. Having experienced so much myself, and having experienced so much vicariously through listening to others' stories, I had seen what worked, and what hadn't.

The description of this incident, written above, does not accurately describe my state of mind at the time. It did not need to – as an incident report its purpose was only to present an effaced narrative of the events.

What really happened was, Pat and Blake began running after the runaway girl. She started running, too, and I followed, running. After a moment or two, I realized that Pat and Blake were not going to

116

catch up with her anytime soon. I also knew that staff members chasing her would only make the girl run faster. She was panicked, and being chased with the realistic possibility of escape would cause her to panic and flee even moreso.

So after that moment or two, I stopped running. Pat and Blake continued on after the girl, and I walked back to the camp van. I walked because, in the grand scheme of things, ten seconds would not necessarily have made much of a difference in this case, and it would not do to injure myself tripping over a rock.

Once I dropped Blake off right near her, the girl realized it was hopeless, and stopped.

It was once this mini-crisis ended that I began to become very introspective about how, over the course of my camp career, I had responded to various camp emergencies. Now that I had seen so many, I almost expected them, and I did not feel the waves of panic that I might have felt earlier in my camp career, or that I observed other, younger, staff members exhibiting.

***

It was years later, when taking a class in Political Leadership at the Maxwell School of Citizenship and Public Affairs, part of Syracuse University, that I was first exposed to the four-types-of-crises model. Type I crises, what might be called a "creeping crisis," results in decentralization – there is not a contraction of authority in the organization (*see* Paul 't Hart, et al., "Crisis Decision Making: The Centralization Thesis Revisited," in *Administration & Society*, 25 no. 1 (1993): 12-44). I recognize that the phrase "creeping crisis" is sometimes used in a derogatory fashion – to deride an organization that does not see a crisis coming. In the context of this work, however, I use it merely to describe a long-term, expected trend that might be styled a crisis or emergency.

A decent example of this might be the conflict with Camp Iroquois (*see* Chapter 2). Though each incident was a short-term crisis, over the course of a summer or two the overall tensions with the rival camp increased in the form of a creeping crisis. Informal and formal delegation occurred: the former when a staff member was caught off-guard in a situation with the other camp and had an opportunity, wanted or unwanted, to set the next waypoint in the inter-camp policy line of trajectory.

An example in the non-camp context might be seen in a city-wide emergency – an outbreak of disease, for example. A well-prepared municipality will have procedures in place to respond to these types of emergencies (like Camp Cory's Code Red), but will decentralize activity, trusting that each department is qualified to handle its prescribed tasks.

I hope that this short treatment proves helpful to the would-be responder to a camp crisis. Whether the crisis is short term or long term, expected or unexpected, and whether the responder is a highest leader with years of experience or a first-time responder, taking a breath, keeping a level head, and remembering training, if any, is a good first step towards responding effectively. And if any mistakes are made, remembering them is beneficial if one is to effectively manage a crisis in the future.

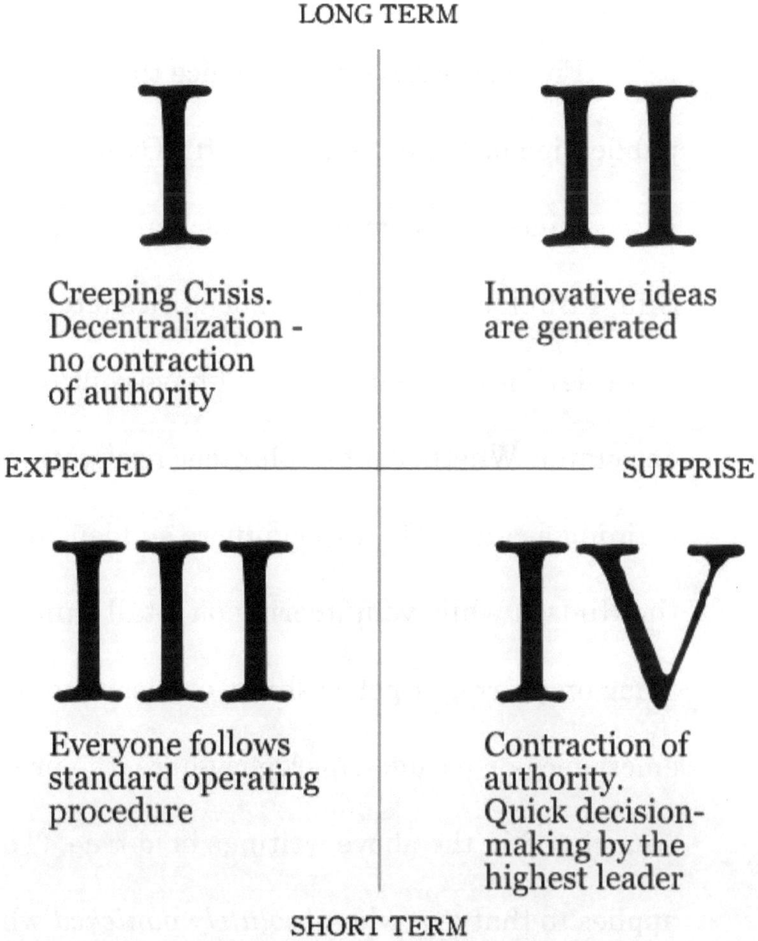

LONG TERM

I Creeping Crisis. Decentralization - no contraction of authority	**II** Innovative ideas are generated
III Everyone follows standard operating procedure	**IV** Contraction of authority. Quick decision-making by the highest leader

EXPECTED ——————————————— SURPRISE

SHORT TERM

Afterword

Five years have passed since the digital publication of "Attention All Staff!" Over a decade has passed since I was employed seasonally at Camp Cory. Still, I think of this collection of stories often, because it is relevant to situations that I have continued to encounter. Whether it be volunteer firefighting, training as an EMT, responding to sudden storms on the Hudson while volunteering on a tall ship, riding along on overnight police shifts, or insert-name-of-emergency-or-pseudo-emergency-here, the principles enunciated in the above writings hold true. (This even applies to that guy who *absolutely panicked* when trying to direct cars into a parking lot that time). I've had friends relate this to me as well. "My brother was injured in a cycling accident," one said. "I was rushing and was going to speed to get to him, but I remembered your book and I walked and took it slowly." Good. One less road accident caused by panicking *a la* the wife in the film version of *Slaughterhouse-Five*.

I've made a few grammatical and formatting changes for the paperback edition (most notably, moving the word "only" where necessary). Much thanks, again, to Dave Ghidiu, who helped with the formatting and publication efforts.

Rereading all of these chapters made me realize that I am older. I am wiser (hopefully not too wise). But, like, seriously dude: what the hell is with Camp Iroquois?

This book is set in Century Schoolbook, a
member of the Century Family of
typefaces. Century is so renowned for its
legibility that the Supreme Court of the
United States mandates that all its briefs
and opinions be set in the Century family.
Century Schoolbook in particular seems
to have been developed in 1918 or 1919.
Some consider it superior to Times New
Roman, when books are concerned,
because Times New Roman was originally
developed by The *Times* of London for
newspapers, which have notoriously
narrow columns. On the other hand
Century fonts, and Century Schoolbook in
particular, are designed for retention
rather than merely for the "quick read."

L.o.C.C.

II.

About the Author

Bo Shoemaker is from Brighton, New York, and obtained degrees from SUNY Geneseo (B.A. – History), Fordham University (M.A. – History), Syracuse University College of Law (J.D.), and Buffalo Law School (LL.M. – Criminal Law). He has been an Assistant District Attorney, an Appellate Court Attorney, a volunteer firefighter, an EMT, and an ultramarathoner.

Bo worked for twelve summers at Camp Cory as Counselor, Waterfront Coordinator, Maijgren Village Head, Leadership Director, Program Director, and eventually Senior Program Director. He currently volunteers as the Camp Historian.